BEI GRIN MACHT SICH IHR
WISSEN BEZAHLT

Bibliografische Information der Deutschen Nationalbibliothek:

Die Deutsche Bibliothek verzeichnet diese Publikation in der Deutschen National-
bibliografie; detaillierte bibliografische Daten sind im Internet über http://dnb.d-
nb.de/ abrufbar.

Impressum:

Copyright © 2014 GRIN Verlag, Open Publishing GmbH
Druck und Bindung: Books on Demand GmbH, Norderstedt Germany
ISBN: 978-3-668-07046-2

Dieses Buch bei GRIN:

http://www.grin.com/de/e-book/308798/taxonomy-of-software-types-a-review-of-
information-systems-and-software

Can Paul Bineytioglu

Aus der Reihe: e-fellows.net stipendiaten-wissen

e-fellows.net (Hrsg.)

Band 1619

Taxonomy of Software Types. A Review of Information Systems and Software Engineering Literature

GRIN Verlag

GRIN - Your knowledge has value

Der GRIN Verlag publiziert seit 1998 wissenschaftliche Arbeiten von Studenten, Hochschullehrern und anderen Akademikern als eBook und gedrucktes Buch. Die Verlagswebsite www.grin.com ist die ideale Plattform zur Veröffentlichung von Hausarbeiten, Abschlussarbeiten, wissenschaftlichen Aufsätzen, Dissertationen und Fachbüchern.

Besuchen Sie uns im Internet:

http://www.grin.com/

http://www.facebook.com/grincom

http://www.twitter.com/grin_com

TAXONOMY OF SOFTWARE TYPES

A LITERATURE REVIEW ON SOFTWARE TYPES
IN THE INFORMATION SYSTEMS AND SOFTWARE ENGINEERING LITERATURE

Master Seminar Paper

submitted: May 2014

by: Can Paul Bineytioglu

Universität Mannheim
Lehrstuhl für ABWL und Wirtschaftsinformatik

Table of Contents

List of Figures

List of Tables

List of Abbreviations

ACM	Association for Computing Machinery
AR	Augmented reality
GIS	Geographical Information System
IS	Information System
IT	Information Technology
RQ	Research question
SMSbIR	Short Message Service based Information
SWEBOK	Software Engineering Body of Knowledge

1 Introduction

Nowadays, more and more problems in business and in everyday life are solved by software. While our grandparents know almost all the streets they live in by heart, our generation uses navigation software on mobile devices to get from one place to another place that is only a few kilometers away. 20 years ago, nobody could imagine such a digital world we are living in today. Probably nobody would believe that a supercomputer, IBM's intelligent *Watson*, would ever beat human beings in the Jeopardy television show.

With considerable improvements and innovations in technology in the recent years, the software industry has seen many changes and has made substantial advancements. New software development techniques, procedures and capabilities have evolved. Also, the variety of types of software products has further diversified and application areas of software both in business and in the private sector have immensely expanded (Park et al., 2003). E.g., real-time data processing applications and software for big data analytics have gained high importance to face the trend of big data in today's business environment.

The increasing number of software types, however, increases the research efforts of researchers as long as newly developed software types are not well classified. Appropriate taxonomies are important in research and practice since the structurization of objects helps researchers and practitioners understand similarities, differences and relationships within complex fields and consequently facilitates research.

Grimshaw (1996) formulated this problem very appropriately:

"The lack of a commonly agreed taxonomy raises the barriers to entry to the subject of information systems and potentially leads to a waste of energies chasing the same thing by a different name. Many disciplines contribute to information systems - this is a healthy state. However, this leads to a tendency for each discipline to use its own framework as the basis of research depending on whether the study has, for example, an organisation, a technology, or a system perspective."

1.1 Goal of the Paper

The goal of this seminar paper is to provide a literature review on the current state of research on software product types in the information systems and software engineering literature. In particular, this paper will provide an overview of currently developed software types by examining existent taxonomies and classification approaches in this field. Additionally, it will be analyzed according to which procedure taxonomies are developed and whether there exists a well-recognized taxonomy development procedure in information systems and software engineering.

The following research questions (RQ) are to be addressed by the literature review:

RQ1:   *What is the state of research on software product types in the Information Systems and Software Engineering literature?*

RQ2:   *What different types of software are developed?*

1.2 Structure of the Paper

Section 2 provides a detailed introduction to the research methodology that will be applied. The research method for the literature review is mainly based on the Systematic Literature Review in Software Engineering approach by Kitchenham (2012). Section 3 addresses the two aforementioned research questions and thereby encompasses the main work of this paper. In particular, the literature search results will be presented (subsection 3.1), a taxonomy development procedure will be discussed and existing taxonomies in IS and software engineering literature will be analyzed. The final section 4 summarizes and concludes the work of this paper and comments on limitations and future research work.

2 Research Methodology

The research methodology that is applied to perform the literature review in this paper is mainly based on Kitchenham's approach of performing a *Systematic Literature Review in Software Engineering* (2012).

The first step is the identification of research, as suggested by Kitchenham (2012). This step comprises identifying a significant number of primary studies relating to the research questions. For the identification process, Kitchenham (2012) suggests a specific search process that will be pursued in this paper. The two key word lists that will be used are shown in table 1 below.

Key Word List 1 (What): Taxonomy	Key Word List 2 (Focus area): Software Types
Taxonomy	Software
Classification	Software products
Categorization	Software applications
Characterization	Software systems
Types	Software tools
	Software types
	Types of software
	Information systems

Table 1: Key Word Lists

The initial search for primary studies was performed by scanning databases with sophisticated search strings, including logical combinations of key words, such as "taxonomy + 'information systems'". Further primary studies were found by searching reference lists from relevant primary studies, as proposed by Kitchenham (2012).

Following electronic databases were primarily used for the literature identification: IEEExplore, ACM Digital Library, Google scholar and Citeseer library.

Table 1 represents the final version of the key word lists. During the process of scanning databases for key word combinations, however, some initially chosen key words proved to be inadequate because they led to too many irrelevant search results (see section 3.1 for detailed search results). Thus, the initial key word lists were iteratively adapted. E.g., "IT systems" was removed from key word list 2, whereas "software tools" was added to the key word list 2.

During the process of finding relevant literature, each study was checked for relevance based on the title and abstract and, in case, added to the literature list. A further investigation of the studies for their relevance was performed in a later step. The relevance of the studies was recorded in the literature list by ranking the studies' relevance from 1 (less relevant) to 3 (highly relevant).

First, all highly relevant studies (rank: 3) were examined, then the medium-relevant, then the less relevant studies.

Additionally, for each study, the number of its occurrences in the overall search results was recorded. E.g., some studies were found through different search queries. Studies that were identified by a high number of search queries were also considered as highly relevant.

3 Literature Review on Software Types in the Information Systems and Software Engineering Literature

In this section, first, the results of the literature search process will be depicted (section 3.1). The subsequent subsections are based on the findings from subsection 3.1. A systematic process of taxonomy development in the information systems field will be presented and the motivation and importance thereof for future research activities in the IS and software engineering field will be outlined (section 3.2). Then, existent taxonomies of software types (section 3.3) and taxonomies of specific domains within the software field (section 3.4) will be reviewed. Finally, the findings of the literature review will be evaluated with regards to the research questions (section 3.5).

3.1 Results of the Literature Search

As already mentioned above, the literature identification focused on the search of the databases IEEExplore, ACM Digital Library, Google scholar and Citeseer library. Additional literature was found through bibliographies of already identified primary literature. Table 2 presents selected results of the database searches.

Key word combination	Searched database	# Search Results
("taxonomy" AND "software")	IEEE[1]	1,344
	ACM[2]	608
("taxonomy" AND "software tools")	IEEE	114
	ACM	18
("taxonomy" AND "information systems")	IEEE	311
	ACM	103
("taxonomy" AND "types of software")	IEEE	4

[1] For searches within the IEEE database, only the metadata was scanned since full text and metadata search resulted in too broad and not target-oriented search results.
[2] For searches within the ACM Digitial Library, the key words were entered under "words or phrases in Abstract" and with the logical operator "AND".

	ACM	3
("classification" AND "software")	IEEE	8,850
	ACM	2,373
("classification" AND "software tools")	IEEE	299
	ACM	54
("classification" AND "information systems")	IEEE	2,840
	ACM	377
("classification" AND "types of software")	IEEE	6
	ACM	7

Table 2: Selected Search Results

With respect to the search results it can be noted that the most precise and relevant papers were found where the number of search results was low. This may be due to the fact that a search with a high number of total search results also yields many irrelevant studies, which makes it difficult to filter the actually relevant studies.

Based on the number of total search results, the key word lists were iteratively adapted. It became evident that searching for the key word combination "classification AND software" was not effective due to the very high number of total search results whereas the search string "classification AND 'types of software'" brought useful results despite only six respectively seven search results.

A thorough analysis of the literature led to following findings:

- There exist only very few taxonomies that extensively encompass diverse software types.

- In contrast to that, there exist a rather high number of taxonomies related to only a specific domain within the IS and software engineering field. This also implies that there is interest in taxonomies in this field.

- Most existent taxonomies do not pursue a taxonomy development process – at least they do not provide any information about the method used.

- Many taxonomies are highly superficial and incomplete having only a few categories and/or dimensions to classify software systems whereas other few papers propose classification schemes with more than ten dimensions.

3.2 Taxonomy Development in the Information Systems Field

Nickerson et al. (2009) propose a method, which is based on the "three-level measurement model" by Bailey (1984), and is assumed to fit for developing taxonomies in the area of information systems. They define a "taxonomy T as a set of n dimensions D_i (i=1, ... , n) each consisting of k_i ($k_i \geq 2$) mutually exclusive and collectively exhaustive characteristics C_{ij} (j=1, ... , k_i) such that each object under consideration has one and only one C_{ij} for each D_i" (Nickerson et al., 2009). Stated another way,

$$T = \{ D_i, i = 1, \dots , n \mid D_i = \{ C_{ij}, j = 1, \dots , k_i , k_i \geq 2 \}\}$$

Additionally, Nickerson et al. (2009) propose following attributes for a useful taxonomy:

- It is *concise* – i.e. it comprises a limited number of dimensions as well as a limited number of characteristics within a dimension.

- It is *sufficiently inclusive* – i.e. it includes a sufficient number of dimensions and characteristics to be interesting.

- It is *comprehensive* – i.e. all objects under study can be classified.

- It is *extendible* – i.e. it is dynamic and can be extended by additional dimensions and characteristics.

- It is *explanatory* – i.e. the dimensions and characteristics provide useful explanations of the nature of the objects under consideration.

Nickerson et al. (2009) also propose five *qualities* of a taxonomy development method that will not be discussed within the scope of this paper.

The complexity and scope of the software field proves taxonomies, classification schemes and any types of structurization to be useful to understand similarities, differences and relationships among objects under study, e.g. software types.

Nickerson et al. (2009) found out that there is a high interest in taxonomies, but formal procedures are barely used. Nickerson et al. (2007) state that a taxonomy could also lead to the design and development of new software systems or applications that fit in the voids identified by the taxonomy. This is particularly considerable with regards to more specific application domains.

Appropriate taxonomies are important in research and practice since the structurization of objects helps researchers and practitioners understand similarities and relationships within complex fields. The reduction of complexity and the identification of relationships among objects under study are major advantages leveraged by taxonomies (Bailey, 1994). E.g., in biology a significant amount of taxonomies have been developed in order to structure the complex world of living organisms and provide a foundation for biological research (Nickerson, Muntermann, Varshney, & Isaac, 2009).

As a set of defined contructs or as a vocabulary of a discipline, taxonomies can be considered as part of a domain's knowledge base and serve as a basis for future research approaches (Hevner et al., 2004; March and Smith, 1995). According to Williams et al. (2008), classification schemes furthermore facilitate the understanding the science behind design principles of artifacts observed. Orlikowski and Iacono (2001) relate this to IS discipline in particular and emphasize the need for understanding the design principles about IT artifacts.

In the software field and particularly in the information systems domain the importance of classification schemes is well recognized (Nickerson et al., 2009). This becomes evident by the number of taxonomies that have been proposed in this field. However, only little has been written about the process of developing a taxonomy in the information systems field (Nickerson et al., 2009), whereas this has been studied in a number of other disciplines, e.g. Bailey (1994) in sociology.

Based on the aforementioned motivation and importance of taxonomies in the software field, it can be argued that there is need for a systematic method for developing taxonomies in the software field respectively information systems field in particular,

which would lay the basis for developing new taxonomies that could bring structure to
complex domains and potentially lead to new research directions (Nickerson et al.,
2009). In this context, Nickerson et al. (2009) draw the conclusion that "taxonomies are
useful in information systems and [...] a formal taxonomy development procedure that
others use in their research would benefit the discipline."

3.3 Taxonomies of Software Types in the Information Systems and Software Engineering Literature

In this section, existent taxonomies of software types in generel as well as taxonomies
of specific domains within the area of information systems and software engineering are
presented and discussed. The following table 3 provides an overview of the studies that
will be examined within this section, indicating the reference (i.e. the author(s)) and the
domain which the proposed taxonomy is categorized to.

In the course of a sophisticated literature search some studies older than 20 years were
found. In the last 20 years, the software field has experienced fundamental changes due
to technological evolution. Thus, examining such "out-dated" studies and taxonomies is
considered unreasonable. Examples for such studies are those published by Doke and
Barrier (1994), Glass and Vessey (1992), Houghton R.C. (1983), Olivier and von Solms
(1994), Mentzas (1994), David J Grimshaw (1992).

Domain of Proposed Taxonomy	Reference	Comment
Software Types (in general)	• GoogleCode • SourceForge • ACM Classification System • Forward and Lethbridge (2008)	Forward and Lethbridge (2008) propose an all-encompassing taxonomy of software types developed based on the other three mentioned sources.
Software	• Software Engineering Body	Only the SWEBOK

Engineering Tools	of Knowledge (Bourque & Dupuis, 2004) • Roongkaew and Prompoon (2013) • Iivari et al. (1999) • Houghton (1983)	taxonomy will be presented since the taxonomy by Roongkaew and Prompoon focuses on software development and the taxonomy by Iivari et al. focuses on information systems development methodologies, which are not the focus of this paper. The study of Houghton (1983) is considered too old.
Software Testing Tools	• Mustafa et al. (2009)	
Geographical Information Systems (GIS)	• Grimshaw (1996)	Several studies proposing a taxonomy of GIS were found in literature. However, they will not be examined in this paper since they were all published before 1996 and are considered "outdated".
Augmented Reality Applications	• Milgram and Colquhoun (1999) • Suomela and Lehikoinen (2004) • Hugues et al. (2011) • Brockmann et al. (2013)	Only the taxonomy by Brockmann et al. (2013) will be presented as it is both the most recent and most comprehensive taxonomy of AR applications.

Global Information Sharing Systems	• Bright et al. (1992)	
Mobile Applications	• Kemper and Wolf (2002) • Leem et al. (2004) • Nysveen et al. (2005) (mobile services) • Heinonen and Pura (2006) (mobile services) • Nickerson et al. (2007) • Dombroviak and Ramnath (2007)	The importance of taxonomies of mobile applications recognized by Lehmann and Lehner (2002) and Okazaki (2005). Dombroviak and Ramnath (2007) focus on pervasive systems. Their taxonomy will not be presented in this paper.
Ambient Information Systems	• McCrickard et al. (2003) • Matthews et al. (2004) • Pousman and Stasko (2006)	

Table 3: Overview of Taxonomies

In addition to the taxonomies listed in the table 3, following selected taxonomies should be mentioned, but will not be analyzed due to scope contraints of this paper:

- Yuan and Malek (2012):   Self-protecting Software Systems

- Joshi and Pathak (2011):   Short Message Service based Information (SMSbIR) Systems

- Dustdar (1997):   Multimedia Information Systems Applications

- Xu et al. (2009):   Software Visualization Tools

With regards to the particular domains of the studies indicated in the table 3, it becomes evident that most taxonomies present in the information systems and software engineering literature focus on highly specific areas rather than providing an all-encompassing taxonomy of all possible software types. Only few approaches to a comprehensive classification scheme of software types exist.

3.3.1 Taxonomies of Software Types in General

The ACM Computing Classification System[3] is widely recognized as the de facto standard classification system for the computing field and comprises a meaningful categorization of technology-related topics. It was last updated in 2012. Its focus is not to serve as a taxonomy of software types. In particular, not only software types, but also software properties, software system structures, system architectures and more are classified within the same taxonomy. Furthermore, the classification schemes for certain domains, such as system software (e.g. operating systems), consumer-oriented systems (e.g. entertainment systems) and information display (e.g. geographical information systems such as maps) are not extensively covered. However, it encompasses classifications and lists of software domains and is therefore relevant with regards to the research questions.

Another disadvantage of the ACM Computing Classification System that arises from the fact that software types, system structures and architectures are classified within the same classification system is that the leaf nodes of the classification tree are not mutually exclusive and exhaustive, e.g. a software type is associated with a system structure and a system architecture and cannot be distinctly classified. This contradicts the definition of a taxonomy by Nickerson et al. (see section 3.2).

In the open-source community, the websites of SourceForge and GoogleCode each provide a useful software type classification system.

The most recent research on the development of an all-encompassing taxonomy of software types was conducted by Forward and Lethbridge (2008). They have faced the problem of the lack of an all-encompassing taxonomy of software types in 2008 and made the attempt to develop such a taxonomy of software types. Their paper's purpose was to develop a taxonomy that "should help researchers to apply their research systematically to particular types of software" (Forward & Lethbridge, 2008).

---

[3] http://www.acm.org/about/class/2012; The ACM Computing Classification System will not furthermore be explained within the scope of this paper. It is publicly accessible via the provided website.

Their work is based on Glass and Vessey (1992) who have formalized the need and justification for a software taxonomy in 1992. Forward and Lethbridge (2008) use a systematic taxonomy development process to cover all contemporary types of software. They consider input from both published studies and experts, iterative review and editing of the results by co-authors (Forward & Lethbridge, 2008). Their taxonomy aims at enabling both researchers and practitioners to perform tasks such as "cataloguing, filing or searching for applications. The taxonomy will also facilitate tagging of components and techniques according to the application types for which they are suitable." (Forward & Lethbridge, 2008)

In particular, they followed following multi-step process to develop the taxonomy:

1. Seed the process with existing taxonomies

2. Conduct multiple tool-supported individual brainstorming sessions

3. Merge the brainstorm results to form a full first draft

4. Refine the taxonomy by applying systematic criteria for subdivision

5. Review and edit the result iteratively

Primary software practitioners, such as software organizations, IT departments within the Canadian federal government and software consulting firms, were requested for input data. The taxonomy was initially based on existing partial taxonomies from ACM, IEEE, GoogleCode and SourceForge and was extended and reviewed by the input received from the software practitioners. In total, 78 sources were considered to develop the resulting taxonomy.

The first two levels of the taxonomy are presented hereinafter. The entire taxonomy can be found in Appendix A.

A Data-dominant software

    A.con Consumer-oriented software

    A.bus Business-oriented software

    A.des Design and engineering software

    A.inf Information display and transaction entry

B Systems software

    B.os Operating systems

    B.net Networking / Communications

    B.dev Device / Peripheral drivers

    B.ut Support utilities

    B.mid Middleware and system components

    B.bp Software Backplanes (e.g. Eclipse)

    B. svr Servers

    B.mal Malware

C Control-dominant software

    C.hw Hardware control

    C.em Embedded software

    C.rt Real-time control software

    C.pc Process control software (i.e. air traffic control, industrial process)

D Computation-dominant software

    D.or Operations research

    D.im Information management and manipulation

    D.art Artistic creativity

    D.sci Scientific software

    D.ai Artificial intelligence

The taxonomy by Forward and Lethbridge (2008) is the only recent approach of an extensive all-encompassing taxonomy of software types. As stated earlier, the other taxonomies found in the literature focus on more specific domains within the software and/or information systems and software engineering field (see table 3).

3.3.2 Taxonomies of Specific Software Systems and Applications

This section presents selected taxonomies of specific software systems or applications, respectively the approaches of the taxonomy development.

Taxonomy of software engineering tools based on the Software Engineering Body of Knowledge (SWEBOK) (Bourque & Dupuis, 2004)

The SWEBOK is a guide in which the IEEE Computer Society established a baseline for the body of knowledge for the field of software engineering. Based on the SWEBOK, software engineering tools can be classified as depicted in figure 1.

| Software requirements tools |
| Software design tools |
| Software construction tools |
| Software testing tools |
| Software maintenance tools |
| Software engineering process tools |
| Software quality tools |
| Software configuration management tools |
| Software engineering management tools |
| Miscellaneous tool issues |

Figure 1: Types of Software Engineering Tools based on SWEBOK

Taxonomy of Software Testing Tools by Mustafa et al. (2009)

Mustafa et al. argue that software products can be classified based on different criteria, e.g. intended usage, complexity, development technology. In their paper, they classified software products based on their intended usage. The resulting software types are the following ones: Web Application (63 tools), Network Protocol (27 tools), Application

Software (18 tools), Java Software (16 tools), Open Source Software (10 tools), Database (7 tools), System Software (2 tools) and Embedded Software (2 tools).

Mustafa et al. (2009) collected 135 software testing tools from the internet and classified them into the categories listed above. The numbers after the software types indicate how many out of the 135 tools were classified to the corresponding software type. However, the study does not clearly specify according to which criteria the tools have been selected.

Nevertheless, the huge differences in the numbers may be meaningful with regards to the feasibility of a taxonomy: Since approximately half of the software testing tools from the internet were classified as *web application* – assumably due to the fact that the tools were collected from the *web* – the software type *web application* could further be differentiated and split into more specific subcategories. Analogously, this can be done for the software type *Network Protocol (27 tools)* and maybe even for more software types.

Taxonomy of geographical information systems by Grimshaw (1996)

Grimshaw critically reviews the recent (i.e. 1996 and previous years) literature on information systems taxonomies, explores the applicability of existent information systems taxonomies to geographical information systems (GIS) and proposes an own taxonomy specifically for GIS. Although this study is almost 20 years old and its relevance to contemporary GIS is doubtful, it will briefly be presented since no recent taxonomy on GIS could be found.

Grimshaw develops a taxonomy that uses a three dimensional framework in order to provide a classification system that reflects a dynamic environment (1996). The three dimensions are: *Decision* dimension, *Technology* dimension and *Strategy* dimension. The *Decision* dimension determines the kind of decisions that need to be made, what data is required, how the data will be used and who will make the decision. Subclasses on this dimension refer to the decision type, i.e. structured, unstructured, and the level of the decision, i.e. strategic tactical or operational (Grimshaw, 1996). The *Technology* and *Strategy* dimensions will not be explained as this would distract from the focus of this paper.

Taxonomy of augmented reality (AR) applications by Brockmann et al. (2013)

In literature, several approaches to classify and structure AR applications exist for particular domains, each serving a specific purpose – e.g. the studies of following authors: Milgram and Colquhoun (1999), Suomela and Lehikoinen (2004), Hugues et al. (2011). The classification approaches differ in terms of used dimensions and the classification criteria.

A more comprehensive and universal taxonomy, however, was only proposed by Brockmann et al. (2013). The following figure illustrates the classification framework.

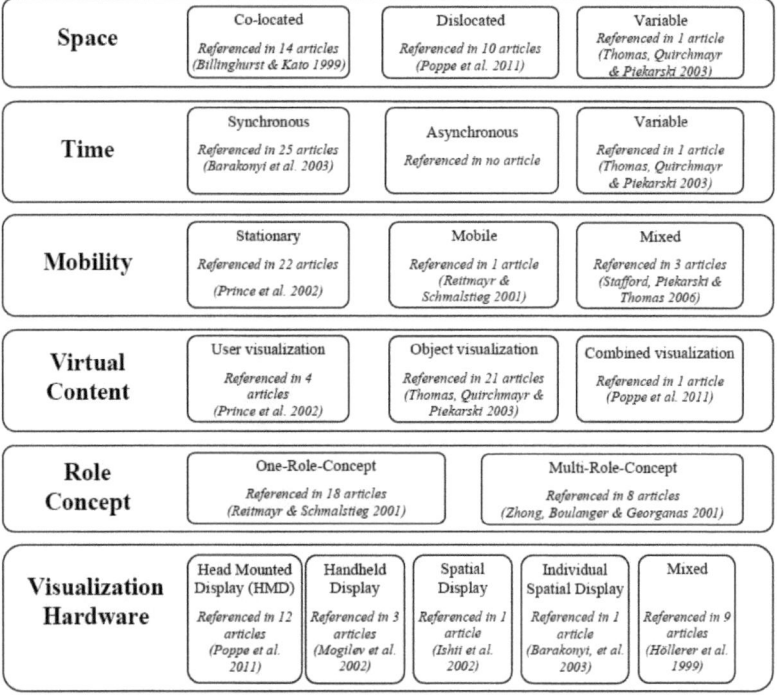

Figure 2: Taxonomy of Collaborative AR Applications by Brockmann et al. (2013)

The classification framework consists of the dimensions space, time, mobility, virtual content, role concept and visualization hardware and thus considers both traditional and AR-specific dimensions for the classification (Brockmann et al., 2013). Furthermore,

this classification framework is one of the few taxonomies that are based on the
taxonomy development method proposed by Nickerson et al. (2009).

Taxonomy of multidatabase systems by Bright et al. (1992)

In literature, a variety of terms exist to describe solutions for global information sharing
in a distributed system, such as distributed databases, multidatabases, federated
databases and interoperable systems. A distributed system for global information
sharing has a global component to access globally shared information and various local
components (Bright et al., 1992).

The taxonomy proposed by Bright et al. classifies global information sharing systems
according to how tightly the global system integrates the local database management
systems. According to Bright et al., a tightly coupled system is characterized by the fact
that global functions have access to low-level internal functions of the local database
management system. The taxonomy is shown in figure 3. The taxonomy comprises
following classes: *distributed database*, *global schema multidatabase*, *federated
database*, *multidatabase language system*, *homogeneous multidatabase language
system*, and *interoperable system*.

Class	Level of Global Interface to Local DBMS	Local Node Types	Full Global Database Function	Method of Global Integration
Distributed database	Internal DBMS functions	Homogeneous databases	Yes	Global schema
Global schema multidatabase	DBMS user interface	Heterogeneous databases	Yes	Global schema
Federated database	DBMS user interface	Heterogeneous databases	Yes	Partial global schemas
Multidatabase language system	DBMS user interface	Heterogeneous databases	Yes	Access language functions
Homogeneous multidatabase language system	DBMS user interface plus some internal DBMS functions	Homogeneous databases	Yes	Access language functions
Interoperable systems	Application on top of the DBMS	Any data source that meets the communication protocol	No	No global integration

Figure 3: Taxonomy of Global Information Sharing Systems by Bright et al. (1992)

According to the taxonomy of Bright et al. (1992),

- A *distributed database* is the most tightly coupled global information sharing
  system as global and local functions share low-level internal interfaces and are
  highly tightly integrated.

- *Global schema multidatabases* are more loosely coupled than distributed databases because local information is accessed through the external user interface of the local database management system. Since the global system component employs a global schema, the local systems have to cooperate closely in order to maintain the global schema.

- *Federated databases* are more loosely coupled than global schema multidatabases. Each local component employs a local import and export schema rather than an overall global schema.

- *Multidatabase language systems* are more loosely coupled than federated databases since no global schema is maintained. *Homogeneous multidatabase language systems* are a subset of multidatabase language systems as there exist numerous multidatabase projects that only support homogeneous local database management systems.

- *Interoperable systems* are the most loosely coupled systems. The global function is only capable of simple data exchange and does not fully support database functionality.

Taxonomy of mobile applications

In recent years, the number and variety of mobile applications have immensely increased. New mobile applications appear regularly (Nickerson, Varshney, Muntermann, & Isaac, 2007). The rapidly expanding range of mobile applications makes it difficult for academia, industry and users to determine whether a new mobile application fits with existing mobile application types, is entirely new, a considerable variation of an existing application or an application of a type that already exists (Nickerson et al., 2007).

The importance of taxonomies in the field of mobile commerce and mobile business research has been well recognized (Lehmann and Lehner, 2002; Okazaki, 2005). However, only a small number of taxonomies of mobile applications have been developed and literature lacks taxonomies in this field that could stimulate future research work (Nickerson et al., 2007).

Kemper and Wolf (2002) develop a classification scheme that is based on the three dimensions *degree of innovation*, *speed of development* and *risk*, and characteristics that are related to mobile application development. However, the taxonomy only refers to the application development process and does not particularly take the specific characteristics of mobile applications into account.

Leem et al. (2004) propose a hierarchical classification scheme based on mobile business models. On the top layer of the classification scheme, they distinguish Business-to-Consumer and Business-to-Business business models. In the lower levels, these nodes are further divided into subcategories. However, the taxonomy by Leem et al. does not serve as a general mobile application classification since it focusus on a particular perspective (i.e. that of mobile business models). Overall, the classification scheme facilitates researchers and practitioners to categorize mobile applications from a business model perspective and can therefore also be considered as a foundation for mobile business model-oriented reseach.

In terms of mobile services, Nysveen et al. (2005) as well as Heinonen and Pura (2006) each suggest a classification scheme from different perspectives. The classification scheme by Nysveen et al. is two-dimensional and categorizes mobile services by the *type of interactivity* (personal-interactive versus machine-interactive) and *process characteristics* (goal-oriented versus experimental). Since these categories represent the entire classification scheme, its descriptiveness can be considered weak.

The classification scheme by Heinonen and Pura (2006) is based on the four dimensions *type of consumption*, *context*, *social setting* and *relationship* and adopts a customer-centric perspective. However, they consider their own taxonomy to be industry-specific and therefore recommend to conduct research towards a more generalized classification of mobile applications.

The taxonomy proposed by Nickerson et al. (2007) does not aim to be a final classification scheme, but instead to analyze the dimensions and categories of mobile applications that could lead to a comprehensive taxonomy of mobile applications.

They suggest following candidate dimensions of a taxonomy where the dimensions characterize the interaction between the user and the mobile application (Nickerson et al., 2007):

Dimension	Categories
Temporal dimension	Synchronous, Asynchronous
Communication dimension	Informational, Reporting, Interactional
Transaction dimension	Transactional, Non-transactional
Public dimension	Public, Private
Multiplicity (or participation) dimension	Individual, Group
Location dimension	Location-based, Non-location-based
Identity dimension	Identity-based, Non-identity-based

Table 4: Dimensions of a Mobile Application Taxonomy by Nickerson et al. (2007)

For example, mobile auctions would be classified as follows: synchronous, interactional, transactional, public, group, non-location-based, identity-based (Nickerson et al., 2007).

Taxonomy of ambient information systems

Before examining taxonomies of ambient information systems, the term of such will be defined. Pousman and Stasko (2006) define an *ambient information system* by its behavioral characteristics:

- Display information that is important but not critical,

- Can move from the periphery to the focus of attention and back again,

- Focus on the tangible representations in the environment,

- Provide subtle changes to reflect updates in information,

- Are aesthetically pleasing and environmentally appropriate.

McCrickard et al. (2003) propose a classification scheme based on the three dimensions *interruption, reaction,* and *comprehension.*

Matthews et al. (2004) develops a taxonomy based on the dimensions *notification level, transition* and *abstraction.* They define *notification level* as the relative importance of a specific data stream. A *transition* means a programmatic change to the display based on the data. *Abstraction* is defined as the mapping that takes some numerical or ordinal data and transforms it into data in a form so that it can be used by the ambient display.

The *notification level* is further subcategorized into *Ignore, Change Blind, Make Aware, Interrupt* and *Demand Attention* (Matthews et al., 2004). The categories of *transition* are: *Interrupt, Make Aware* and *Change Blind. Abstraction* is split into *Feature Abstraction* and *Degradation.*

Pousman and Stasko (2006) develop the most recent taxonomy of ambient information systems. They propose four design dimensions: *Information capacity, notification level, representational fidelity, aesthetic emphasis.* The result of applying 19 research systems and three consumer ambient information systems on these dimensions are four design patterns. However, those will not be presented or discussed within this paper as it would distract from the focus of the paper.

4 Summary, Conclusion, Limitations and Future Work

Summary and Conclusion

The goal of this paper was to answer the following two research questions based on a literature review:

> *RQ1: What is the state of research on software product types in the Information Systems and Software Engineering literature?*

> *RQ2: What different types of software are developed?*

The literature review has concluded following findings:

- There exist only very few taxonomies that extensively encompass a wide range of software types.

- In contrast to that, there exist a relatively high number of taxonomies related to a specific domain within the IS and software engineering field. This also implies that there is interest in taxonomies in this field.

- Most existent taxonomies do not pursue a taxonomy development process – at least they do not provide any information about a systematic method used.

- Many taxonomies are highly superficial and incomplete having only a few categories and/or dimensions to classify software systems whereas other few papers propose more sophisticated classification schemes with a high number of dimensions and categories.

From these findings can be inferred that there is high interest in taxonomies for software types of particular domains, such as mobile applications. Contrary to that, there is obviously not much interest in a taxonomy that covers a broad range of software types. Apart from the study by Forward and Lethbridge (2008), publishers of such general taxonomies are organizations (GoogleCode, SourceForge, ACM).

Since Forward and Lethbridge (2008) propose the most recent and most all-encompassing taxonomy of software types, their taxonomy of software types provides the answer to *RQ2*, and consequently the answer to *RQ1* as well.

Due to their coverage of a wide variety of software types, the categories on the lowest level (leaf nodes) are not elaborated in high detail. However, this is not mandatory to answer the research questions. The taxonomies each within a specific domain of the software field are considered complementary to the more general taxonomy by Forward and Lethbridge (2008) in the way that they extend the taxonomy of software types with a higher level of detail.

From a critical point of view, the taxonomy by Forward and Lethbridge (2008) was only cited twice according to the statistics of the ACM Digital Library. This may cast doubt on the usefulness or relevance of the proposed taxonomy in research.

The publication date of a study is another aspect to take into account when analyzing taxonomies in the software field. The year in which a study was published plays an important role since the application areas of software have immensely expanded and a wide range of new types of software have evolved with the advance of computer technology (e.g., mobile applications, cloud computing, real-time applications) (Park et al., 2003).

The development of software types over time affects both (1) software types that have already existed, and (2) entirely new software types that appeared in recent years. Examples of software types of category (1) amongst others could be data management systems, information storage systems and security and privacy systems. They have existed since a long time. However, the characteristics and forms of appearance vary when comparing contemporary systems with such from earlier years. E.g., in terms of information storage systems, traditional information storage technologies use magnetic disks, magnetic tapes and disk arrays. In contrast, contemporary storage architectures include cloud based storage technologies and diverse storage management technologies that have not existed many years ago.

Examples of software types of category (2) are mobile applications, cloud-based software on demand, big data analytics software or particular augmented reality applications that, as stated above, have not existed many years ago. It can furthermore be expected that the aforementioned software types will continue to expand in near future and new application areas will appear.

Consequently, a taxonomy of software types as well as taxonomies for certain domains are not long-lasting, but rather ever-changing due to the rapid changes in technology and advancements in the software field. In this context, the following foresight by Jean Sammet in her "President's Letter" of the Communications of the ACM from 1975 suits very well (1975):

"Although I am personally very much in favor of trying to define all terms and provide taxonomies, I think that any attempt to do this for the computing field is doomed to failure at least for the foreseeable future. The field doesn't seem to be mature enough yet to enable us to develop and agree on clearcut technology."

This quote raises the question whether we are mature enough today, after approximately 40 years. The literature review has shown that we are not yet mature.

Limitations

This paper does not contend that all relevant studies related to the research questions were extensively identified and examined, but the most relevant ones to a certain upper limit in the total number of studies. Moreover, the taxonomies considered in this paper were not analyzed for their taxonomy development method. The taxonomies were not evaluated for their usefulness, which could be done in future work based on the attributes of a useful taxonomy defined by Nickerson et al. (2009).

Future Work

The classification approach by Forward and Lethbridge (2008) provides a suitable basis for future work in the area of taxonomies of software types in the information systems and software engineering field. Future research could critically evaluate the usefulness of their taxonomy in both research and practice in order to further develop it and improve it. Based on that work, a de facto standard of a taxonomy of software types could be proposed, such as the ACM Classification System in the computing field. As stated earlier, such a taxonomy would strongly facilitate researchers' and practitioners' work.

It is recommended that future taxonomies in the information systems field take into account the proposed taxonomy development method by Nickerson et al. (2009) in order to ensure a certain quality level of their taxonomy.

Bibliography

Bailey, K. D. (1984). A three-level measurement model. *Quality and Quantity, 18*(3), 225–245. doi:10.1007/BF00156457

Bailey, K. D. (1994). *Typologies and Taxonomies - An Introduction to Classification Techniques*. Thousand Oaks, California: Sage. Retrieved from http://books.google.de/books/about/Typologies_and_Taxonomies.html?id=1TaYul GjhLYC&pgis=1

Bourque, P. and Dupuis, R. (2004). Guide to the Software Engineering Body of Knowledge 2004 Version. *Guide to the Software Engineering Body of Knowledge, 2004. SWEBOK, -*.

Bright, M. W., Hurson, A. R. and Pakzad, S. H. (1992). A taxonomy and current issues in multidatabase systems. *Computer, 25*(3), 50–60. doi:10.1109/2.121509

Brockmann, T., Krueger, N., Stieglitz, S. and Bohlsen, I. (2013). A Framework for Collaborative Augmented Reality Applications. In *Proceedings of the 19th Americas Conference on Information Systems (AMCIS)*. Chicago, USA.

Doke, E. R. and Barrier, T. (1994). An assessment of information systems taxonomies: time to be re-evaluate? *Journal of Information Technology, 9*(2), 149–157. doi:10.1057/jit.1994.15

Dombroviak, K. M. and Ramnath, R. (2007). A taxonomy of mobile and pervasive applications. In *Proceedings of the 2007 ACM symposium on Applied computing - SAC '07* (p. 1609). New York, New York, USA: ACM Press. doi:10.1145/1244002.1244345

Dustdar, S. (1997). Multimedia information systems applications - A taxonomy and three case studies. In *Multimedia Computing and Systems '97. Proceedings., IEEE International Conference on* (pp. 654–655). doi:10.1109/MMCS.1997.609803

Forward, A. and Lethbridge, T. C. (2008). A Taxonomy of Software Types to Facilitate Search and Evidence-based Software Engineering. In *Proceedings of the 2008 Conference of the Center for Advanced Studies on Collaborative Research: Meeting of Minds* (pp. 14:179–14:191). New York, NY, USA: ACM. doi:10.1145/1463788.1463807

Glass, R. L. and Vessey, I. (1992). Toward a taxonomy of software application domains: History. *Journal of Systems and Software, 17*(2), 189–199. doi:10.1016/0164-1212(92)90095-2

Grimshaw, D. J. (1992). Towards a Taxonomy of information systems: or does anyone need a TAXI? *Journal of Information Technology, 7*(1), 30–36. doi:10.1057/jit.1992.5

Grimshaw, D. J. (1996). Towards a taxonomy of geographical information systems. In *System Sciences, 1996., Proceedings of the Twenty-Ninth Hawaii International Conference on ,* (Vol. 3, pp. 547–556 vol.3). doi:10.1109/HICSS.1996.493250

Heinonen, K. and Pura, M. (2006). Developing a Conceptual Framework for Mobile Services. *Proceedings of the Helsinki Mobility Roundtable 2006.*

Hevner, A. R., March, S. T., Park, J. and Ram, S. (2004). Design science in information systems research. *MIS Quarterly, 28*(1), 75–105. Retrieved from http://dl.acm.org/citation.cfm?id=2017212.2017217

Houghton R.C., J. (1983). Software Development Tools: A Profile. *Computer, 16*(5), 63–70. doi:10.1109/MC.1983.1654382

Hugues, O., Fuchs, P. and Nannipieri, O. (2011). *New Augmented Reality Taxonomy: Technologies and Features of Augmented Environment.* (B. Furht, Ed.). New York, NY: Springer New York. doi:10.1007/978-1-4614-0064-6

Iivari, J., Hirschheim, R. and Klein, H. K. (1999). Beyond methodologies: keeping up with information systems development approaches through dynamic classification. In *Systems Sciences, 1999. HICSS-32. Proceedings of the 32nd Annual Hawaii International Conference on* (Vol. Track7, p. 10 pp.–). doi:10.1109/HICSS.1999.772825

Joshi, M. R. and Pathak, V. M. (2011). A functional taxonomy of SMSbIR systems. In *Electronics Computer Technology (ICECT), 2011 3rd International Conference on* (Vol. 6, pp. 166–171). doi:10.1109/ICECTECH.2011.5942074

Kemper, H.-G., & Wolf, E. Iterative Process Models for Mobile Application Systems: A Framework, ICIS 2002 Proceedings (2002). Retrieved from http://aisel.aisnet.org/icis2002/37

Kitchenham, B. A. (2012). Systematic review in software engineering. In *Proceedings of the 2nd international workshop on Evidential assessment of software technologies - EAST '12* (p. 1). New York, New York, USA: ACM Press. doi:10.1145/2372233.2372235

Leem, C. S., Suh, H. S. and Kim, D. S. (2004). A classification of mobile business models and its applications. *Industrial Management & Data Systems, 104*(1), 78–87. doi:10.1108/02635570410514115

Lehmann, H. and Lehner, F. Making Sense of Mobile Applications - A Critical Note to Recent Approaches to Their Taxonomy and Classification, BLED 2002 Proceedings (2002). Retrieved from http://aisel.aisnet.org/bled2002/30

March, S. T. and Smith, G. F. (1995). Design and natural science research on information technology. *Decision Support Systems, 15*(4), 251–266. doi:10.1016/0167-9236(94)00041-2

Matthews, T., Dey, A. K., Mankoff, J., Carter, S. and Rattenbury, T. (2004). A toolkit for managing user attention in peripheral displays. In *Proceedings of the 17th annual ACM symposium on User interface software and technology - UIST '04* (p. 247). New York, New York, USA: ACM Press. doi:10.1145/1029632.1029676

McCrickard, D. S., Chewar, C. M., Somervell, J. P. and Ndiwalana, A. (2003). A model for notification systems evaluation---assessing user goals for multitasking activity. *ACM Transactions on Computer-Human Interaction, 10*(4), 312–338. doi:10.1145/966930.966933

Mentzas, G. (1994). A functional taxonomy of computer-based information systems. *International Journal of Information Management, 14*(6), 397–410. doi:10.1016/0268-4012(94)90015-9

Mustafa, K. M., Al-Qutaish, R. E. and Muhairat, M. I. (2009). Classification of Software Testing Tools Based on the Software Testing Methods. In *Computer and Electrical Engineering, 2009. ICCEE '09. Second International Conference on* (Vol. 1, pp. 229–233). doi:10.1109/ICCEE.2009.9

Nickerson, R., Muntermann, J., Varshney, U. and Isaac, H. (2009). *TAXONOMY DEVELOPMENT IN INFORMATION SYSTEMS: DEVELOPING A TAXONOMY OF MOBILE APPLICATIONS*. Retrieved from http://halshs.archives-ouvertes.fr/halshs-00375103

Nickerson, R., Varshney, U., Muntermann, J. and Isaac, H. Towards a Taxonomy of Mobile Applications, AMCIS 2007 Proceedings (2007). Retrieved from http://aisel.aisnet.org/amcis2007/338

Nysveen, H., Pedersen, P. E. and Thorbjørnsen, H. (2005). Intentions to Use Mobile Services: Antecedents and Cross-Service Comparisons. *Journal of the Academy of Marketing Science, 33*(3), 330–346. doi:10.1177/0092070305276149

Okazaki, S. (2005). New perspectives on m-commerce research. *Journal of Electronic Commerce Research, 6*(3), 160–164.

Olivier, M. S. and von Solms, S. H. (1994). A taxonomy for secure object-oriented databases. *ACM Transactions on Database Systems, 19*(1), 3–46. doi:10.1145/174638.174640

Orlikowski, W. J. and Iacono, C. S. (2001). Research Commentary: Desperately Seeking the "IT" in IT Research—A Call to Theorizing the IT Artifact. Retrieved from http://pubsonline.informs.org/doi/abs/10.1287/isre.12.2.121.9700?journalCode=isre

Park, D., Oh, J., Lee, J., Lee, B. and Wu, C. (2003). Quality certification based on hierarchical classification of software packages. In *Science and Technology, 2003. Proceedings KORUS 2003. The 7th Korea-Russia International Symposium on* (Vol. 2, pp. 148–154 vol.2).

Paul Milgram, H. C. J. (1999). A Taxonomy of Real and Virtual World Display Integration. Retrieved from http://citeseer.uark.edu:8080/citeseerx/viewdoc/summary?doi=10.1.1.32.6230

Pousman, Z. and Stasko, J. (2006). A taxonomy of ambient information systems: Four patterns of design. *In Proceedings of the ACM Conference on Advanced Visual Interfaces 2006*, 67–74. Retrieved from http://citeseerx.ist.psu.edu/viewdoc/summary?doi=10.1.1.92.6078&rank=6

Roongkaew, W. and Prompoon, N. (2013). Software engineering tools classification based on SWEBOK taxonomy and software profile. In *Informatics and Applications (ICIA),2013 Second International Conference on* (pp. 122–128). doi:10.1109/ICoIA.2013.6650241

Sammet, J. (1975). President's Letter. *Communications of the ACM, 18*(12).

Suomela, R. and Lehikoinen, J. (2004). Taxonomy for visualizing location-based information. *Virtual Reality, 8*(2), 71–82. doi:10.1007/s10055-004-0139-8

Williams, K., Chatterjee, S. and Rossi, M. (2008). Design of emerging digital services: a taxonomy. *European Journal of Information Systems, 17*(5), 505–517. doi:10.1057/ejis.2008.38

Xu, S., Chen, X. and Liu, D. (2009). Classifying software visualization tools using the Bloom's taxonomy of cognitive domain. In *Electrical and Computer Engineering, 2009. CCECE '09. Canadian Conference on* (pp. 13–18). doi:10.1109/CCECE.2009.5090082

Yuan, E. and Malek, S. (2012). A taxonomy and survey of self-protecting software systems. In *Software Engineering for Adaptive and Self-Managing Systems (SEAMS), 2012 ICSE Workshop on* (pp. 109–118). doi:10.1109/SEAMS.2012.6224397

Appendix A

<u>Taxonomy of software types by Forward and Lethbridge (2008)</u>

A Data-dominant software
  A.con Consumer-oriented software
    1 Communication and information
      a Voice
      b Text / Chat
      c. Email
      d Web browsers
      e. Personal Information management (calendaring, address book)
      f. File / document sharing (i.e. FTP)
    2. Productivity and creativity
      a. Text Editors
      b. Word processing
      c. Spreadsheets / Calculators
      d. Presentation (e.g. PowerPoint)
      e. Desktop Publishing
      f. Personal time management
    3. Entertainment and education
      a. Learning and Reference
      b. Training / Courseware
      c. E-Books
      d. Photo / video / music management (e.g. iLife)
      e. Media players (e.g. music, graphics, photo etc)

f. Movies / Animations / Audio (as software as opposed to pure data or players)
g. Games
4. Personal management
   a. Genealogy
   b. Personal finance / budgeting
   c. Personal will / legal assistance software
   d. Tax preparation / planning
   e. Monitor / tracking software (e.g. training / health)
A.bus Business-oriented software
   1. Strategic and operations analysis
      a. Statistical / risk analysis
      b. Financial analysis and enterprise resource planning
      c. Legal analysis / assistance
      d. Domain specific database searching (e.g. patent, trademark off-line searches)
      e. Workforce Management (e.g. time and attendance software)
      f. Payroll and human resources management
      g. Project management / workflow
      h. Procurement
      i. Scheduling and logistics
      j Medical diagnosis
   2. Corporate management
      a. Real-estate management
      b. Restaurant management / reservations / meal planning
      c. Sales management
      d. Portfolio management
      e. Hospital management
      f. Facilities management
   3. Information management and decision support systems
      a. Data warehousing
      b. Expert systems
      c. Management information systems
      d. Knowledge / records / information management system
      e. Product support, help desk system
      f. Health information / online medical records
      g. Geographical information systems
      h. Data mining / business intelligence management systems
   4. Transaction processing
      a. Accounting
      b. Payroll
      c. Inventory management
      d. Order management and Billing support
      e. Bank transaction processing
      f. Government tax processing
      g. Transportation reservation (airline, train, bus)
      h. University / school timetabling and registration
      i. Reward program backends
      j. Bulk data analysis

A.des Design and engineering software
   1. Development environment
      a. Implementation tools (i.e. editors, refactoring, code-assist, etc)
      b. Version control / configuration management
      c. Process support tools (i.e. debuggers, context-sensitive help, etc)
      d. Development environment plugins
      e. Software development simulation / prototyping
   2. Compilers / interpreters / disassemblers
   3. Automatic Code Generation
   4. Database, Development, Reporting
   5. CAD / CAE tools
   6. Modeling / CASE tools
   7. Drafting / Architecture tools
   8. CAM (Computer-aided manufacturing) tools
   9. Engineering analysis
   10. Benchmarks
   11. Software testing tools
A.inf Information display and transaction entry
   1. Information resources
      a. Languages (Spoken / Written)
      b. Libraries
      c. Maps & Travelling
      d. Contact information software (e.g. phone book)
   2. Standalone applications for displaying information
   3. Web applications / services
      a. Search engines
      b. News and media
      c. User-generated content (e.g. Blogger, Wordpress, message boards)
      d. Social networking (e.g. Facebook)
      e. Weather
      f. Job search
      g. Maps and navigation
      h. Online dictionaries and encyclopaedias
      i. Online booking (travel, entertainment)
      j. Online productivity software
      k. Website content management
      l Web Authoring / Publishing Software
      m. Public library systems
      n. Enrolment / registration in education
      o. E-Commerce
      p. E-finance (banking, investing, money transfer)
      q. E-Government (passports, birth certificates, vehicle registrations, gun registration, unemployment insurance apps. etc.)
      r. E-Democracy (voting online)

B. Systems software
B.os Operating systems
   1. Accessibility
   2. Administrator software and tools

3. Emulation / emulators
4. Games console operating systems
5. Virtual machines
6. Kernels / distributions (e.g. Linux, Mac, Windows, Palm, QnX)

B.net Networking / Communications

B.dev Device / Peripheral drivers

B.ut Support utilities
1. Anti-virus / anti-spyware / firewalls
2. Authentication tools
3. Backup, Recovery, Storage
4. Compression / decompression
5. Data format conversion
6. Diagnostic / process viewer / activity monitor
7. Disk maintenance
8. Encryption / decryption
9. Failure diagnosis
10. Logging and log analysis
11. Screen capture
12. Network traffic monitor
13. Security
14. Software installer / uninstaller
15. Tunnelled communication network client (e.g. VPN)
16. Wireless Utilities

B.mid Middleware and system components
1. Database servers
2. Graphics packages / rendering engines
3. Interoperability infrastructures
4. UI support software
5. Virtual machines
6. Windowing system servers

B.bp Software Backplanes (e.g. Eclipse)

B.svr. Servers
1. Email servers
2 IM servers
3. Load balancers
4. Proxy servers
5. Web / FTP / Content servers
6. Other daemon processes

B.mal Malware
1. Key loggers
2. Spyware
3. Viruses / Trojans

C. Control-dominant software
  C.hw. Hardware control
1. Firmware (e.g. software in printers, DVDs, watches, fridges, etc)
2. Device control - soft-loadable (e.g. robotics, medical, e-voting, etc)
  C.em. Embedded software
  C.rt. Real time control software

C.pc. Process control software (i.e. air traffic control, industrial process, nuclear plants)

D. Computation-dominant software
  D.or. Operations research
1. Computer science hard problems (i.e. Travelling salesman)
2. Simulation software
  D.im. Information management and manipulation
1. Inventory control
2. Sales forecasting
3. Budget generation / management
4. Search engine processing
  D.art. Artistic creativity
1. Photo, drawing, graphics editing / manipulation
2. Audio & recording, mastering
3. Music composition (audio editing / synthesis)
4. Movie creation (film / movie production)
5. Video processing (editing, surveillance, recognition)
  D.sci Scientific software
1. Idle-time data analysis (e.g. SETi)
2. Simulation software
3. Signal analysis software
4. Image processing
5. Computer Vision
  D.ai Artificial intelligence
1. Agents
2. Machine learning
3. Virtual Reality
4. Robotics / Cybernetics